CONTENTS

About London

London is the capital city of England. Over seven million people live there from all over the world. Its history goes back to Roman times, when there was a town called Londinium on the site.

Greater London

Originally, London was just a village. As it grew and became richer, it spread into many other villages such as Hampstead, Wimbledon and Richmond, which later became part of Greater London.

Hampton Court

Now London stretches from Hampton Court in the West to beyond the Thames Barrier in the East.

The Thames Barrier stops the River Thames from flooding London.

The City

The oldest part of London is called the City. It is on the site of Roman Londinium, which was surrounded by a city wall. It is sometimes called "The Square Mile" because this is approximately the area it covers. The City is now best-known for its financial trading.

Part of the City

The West End

After medieval times, the rich people of London moved out of the City to the west. The West End is still one of the wealthier parts of

London with many expensive shops and houses.

The East End

The East End used to be known as the poorer end of London. This is because the shipping industry and docks there declined early in the twentieth century, so a lot of

people lost their jobs. Now this is changing and it has become an area of small industries and new housing.

Here is a panoramic view of London from a bridge over the River Thames.

Transport

London's Underground railway system is the oldest in the world. It is one of the quickest ways to get around the city.

Look out for the London Transport symbol at bus stops and Underground (Tube) stations.

London's double decker buses give you a good view of the sights.

If you are spending all day in London, you can buy a daily travelpass from Underground stations and some shops. This allows you to use buses and the Underground. You can also buy weekly ones.

A more expensive way to travel is by taxi cab.

A London cab

London through the ages

Roman Londinium was the first major settlement in the Thames Valley, built in the first century AD. Queen Boudicca of a native tribe called the Iceni fought the Romans. She burned Londinium down, but they gradually defeated her.

Queen Boudicca

The Anglo-Saxons

After the Romans had left in the fourth century AD, people called Angles, Saxons and Jutes invaded Britain and established the Anglo-Saxon way of life. Christianity spread and they built many new churches.

Medieval London

After the arrival of Norman kings in 1066, London became busier with churches, street sellers and markets.

The Tudors

The Tudor monarchs reigned between 1485 and 1603. The most famous were Henry VIII and his daughter Elizabeth I. During their time London became a prosperous and powerful city.

Queen Elizabeth I

Oliver Cromwell

In the 1640s Oliver Cromwell tried to overthrow the monarchy. This led to the execution of Charles I in London, but a new king was crowned in 1660.

6

People who caught the plague had to mark their doors with a red cross.

The Great Fire

In 1666 a fire started in Pudding Lane and spread very quickly among the wooden buildings. Much of the city was destroyed. The houses were later rebuilt in brick.

There was a lot of poverty in Victorian times. Many people lived in slums and poor children often had to beg to survive.

The twentieth century

London continued to expand in the twentieth century. New businesses and industries have appeared and people from all over the world have made London their home. It is now a city of many different cultures, traditions and lifestyles.

The Plague

By the seventeenth century London was a packed and filthy city. In 1665 an epidemic of bubonic plague spread rapidly from rats in the docks, killing about 100,000 people.

The growth of London

By the time Queen Victoria came to the throne in 1837 London was becoming the focus of world trade. During her reign, shipbuilding grew and the new railways meant that people could travel around the city more easily. Better street lighting and roads gradually developed too.

The Islamic temple in Regent's Park was built by the Muslim population in London.

Important buildings

London has been the main base for Britain's Government and its Royal Family for centuries. This means that there are plenty of important buildings that are interesting to look at.

The Houses of Parliament

In 1834 the old Palace of Westminster was almost completely destroyed by a fire, so a new one was built in its place.

The clock tower is known as Big Ben, but really Big Ben is the name of the bell inside it.

The Houses of Parliament are known as the Palace of Westminster. This is because kings lived in the old palace until the sixteenth century, when Henry VIII moved out. Ever since then it has been used for government instead.

Inside the House of Commons

There are over 1,000 rooms in the Houses of Parliament. One of the most important is the House of Commons. This is where elected Members of Parliament (MPs), including the Prime Minister, gather to debate new laws.

The Tower of London

The Tower of London was built as a castle and a palace, but it has been used as a zoo, a royal mint and a prison as well. Today you can visit the Tower and see many different sights.

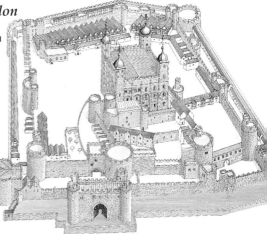

The Crown Jewels are kept in the Jewel House.

Imperial State Crown

The Crown Jewels include a famous Indian diamond, called the Koh-I-Noor, (which means "Mountain of Light"), and the biggest cut diamond in the world, the "Star of Africa".

There is a big collection of weaponry and battle gear in the White Tower.

The guards outside the Tower are called Beefeaters or Yeoman Warders.

Some ravens live around the Tower. The story goes that if they leave, the nation will fall, so their wings are clipped.

Other buildings to spot

All around London there are plaques marking the houses where famous people have lived. They are blue with white lettering, like this one.

LORD ★ HALDANE

The Guildhall is where the Lord Mayor of London is elected. Inside, there are two strange statues of legendary giants, called Gog and Magog.

Magog   *Gog*

Churches and cathedrals

St. Paul's Cathedral is probably London's most famous landmark. Its dome can be seen from many different viewpoints in the city.

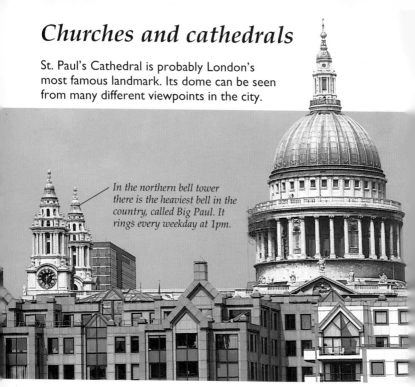

In the northern bell tower there is the heaviest bell in the country, called Big Paul. It rings every weekday at 1pm.

The original cathedral was destroyed in the Great Fire of London in 1666. The architect Sir Christopher Wren was commissioned to redesign it and it took 35 years to build.

Sir Christopher Wren

The big dome has a balcony running around the inside of it called the Whispering Gallery. If you whisper close to the wall, people on the far side of the dome can hear you.

Wartime

During the Second World War, many bombs were dropped around the cathedral. Two of them dropped on St. Paul's itself, but fortunately it was not very badly damaged.

Wren's churches

Sir Christopher Wren designed 23 churches as well as St. Paul's Cathedral. St. Bride's in the City is one of them. The idea for tiered wedding cakes came from the shape of its spire.

St. Bride's Church

St. Martin-in-the-Fields

St. Martin-in-the-Fields is on Trafalgar Square. It was built in 1721. Since then, many copies of it have been built in America.

Lunchtime concerts take place here.

Westminster Abbey

Westminster Abbey is one of the oldest buildings in London. It was founded by King Edward the Confessor, and the original building was finished in 1065.

There are about 1,000 monuments inside the Abbey, commemorating the lives of many kinds of people, such as poets and statesmen.

Shakespeare's memorial

Westminster Abbey

Coronations

Queen Elizabeth II was crowned in Westminster Abbey in 1953.

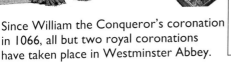

The Coronation Throne

Since William the Conqueror's coronation in 1066, all but two royal coronations have taken place in Westminster Abbey.

Other famous churches

Mark the boxes when you have seen these churches:

St. Mary-le-Bow ☐

St. Clement Danes ☐

Southwark Cathedral ☐

11

Museums and galleries

There are so many things to look at in the London museums that it is a good idea to look at a museum's guidebook and decide what you want to see before you start to go around.

The British Museum

Mummies of a man and a cat

The British Museum has a very big collection of things from ancient civilizations such as Egypt, Greece and Roman Britain. It is particularly famous for its Egyptian mummies.

The Science Museum

At the Science Museum you can learn all sorts of things about science and technology. There are machines and exhibits that you can experiment with yourself.

The Victoria and Albert Museum

This museum (known as the "V and A") has Britain's largest collection of things such as tapestries, costumes and glassware.

A miniature portrait by the Elizabethan artist Nicholas Hilliard, kept at the V and A.

Other museums to visit

Mark the boxes when you have visited these museums:

The Museum of Mankind

Exhibits show life in many different countries.

The Museum of the Moving Image

Find out about the history of television, photography and film.

The Museum of Childhood, Bethnal Green

This museum has the largest collection of toys in the country.

The Museum of London

See how London has developed through the ages.

12

The Natural History Museum

This museum is famous for its huge model animals and dinosaurs. One of them is an enormous model of a blue whale, the biggest animal alive today. You can also see many other plant and animal specimens.

The model blue whale is over 27m (89ft) long.

Madame Tussaud's and the Planetarium

At Madame Tussaud's you can see lifelike wax figures of famous people such as stars, statesmen and criminals. More models are being made all the time. It takes about three months to make each one.

These historical models at Madame Tussaud's are of Henry VIII and his six wives.

The Planetarium is next door to Madame Tussaud's. There you can find out how astronomy has developed over the years and see a spectacular projection of the Universe in a large dome.

The National Gallery

The National Gallery has a valuable collection of paintings by famous artists such as Rembrandt and Van Gogh.

The Tate Gallery

The Tate Gallery is famous for its exhibitions of modern art as well as for its collection of historic British paintings.

Palaces and parks

London's palaces are some of its most famous buildings. They are built in lovely parkland which, with all the other parks, helps to make London one of the most leafy cities in the world.

Buckingham Palace

Buckingham Palace is the Queen's official home. When she is there, the Royal Standard flag flies above the front balcony.

The Royal Standard flag

A view of Buckingham Palace

Every other morning, unless it is very wet, the Guard in front of the palace is changed. You can watch this ceremony from the palace gates.

You can visit the State Apartments of the Palace at certain times of year. The Apartment rooms include the State Dining Room, which can seat 60 guests.

Hampton Court Palace

Hampton Court was built by Henry VIII's chief minister, Cardinal Wolsey, in 1525. He gave it to Henry who lived there with five of his six wives in turn.

Henry VIII

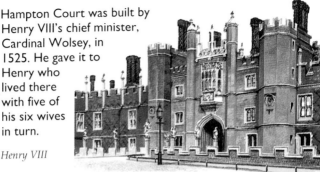

Parks in central London

St. James's Park, Green Park, Regent's Park and Hyde Park are the main parks in central London.

St. James's Park is famous for the birds on its lake, which include pelicans.

Kew Gardens

Kew Gardens has the most famous collection of plants and flowers in the world. Some of them, such as the fly-catching plants, are very strange and exotic.

A Chinese-style pagoda in Kew Gardens

Other parks and open spaces

Mark the boxes when you have visited these places:

Hampstead Heath ☐

Clapham Common ☐

Wimbledon Common ☐

Greenwich Park ☐

Battersea Park ☐

Richmond Park ☐

Richmond Park is famous for its red and fallow deer.

Statues and squares

London's squares are good places to spot interesting statues. Many of them are popular meeting places, too.

The Piazza, Covent Garden

The Piazza was designed by the famous architect Inigo Jones in the 1630s. It was originally surrounded by houses. This idea led to many squares being built throughout London.

The Piazza in the seventeenth century

The clock outside the Swiss Centre in Leicester Square plays a selection of tunes at 12pm, 6pm and 8pm.

Leicester Square

Leicester Square is in the heart of the West End. There are many cinemas, restaurants and clubs around the square. Street performers often gather crowds there. It is also close to Soho and Chinatown, which are always thronged with people.

Statues and squares to spot

Mark the boxes if you see any of these:

St. James's Square ☐

Sloane Square ☐

Statue of Boadicea or Boudicca (see page 6) near Westminster Bridge ☐

Statue of Eros in Piccadilly Circus ☐

Peter Pan

There are fairies, rabbits and fieldmice at the base of Peter Pan's statue.

There is a statue of Peter Pan in Kensington Gardens, by the Long Water. Peter Pan is a fictional character who never grows old. He was created by the writer J. M. Barrie.

16

Trafalgar Square

Trafalgar Square was named after the Battle of Trafalgar in 1805, in which Admiral Lord Nelson led the British fleet to victory over the French. On October 21 each year there is a service under the column to commemorate Nelson.

Nelson's statue is over 5m (16ft) high.

Nelson lost an arm and an eye in battle, so the statue shows him with just one of each.

Nelson's Column

The four bronze lions around the square were cast from the cannon of battleships by the artist Sir Edwin Landseer.

You can see the National Gallery behind the lions.

Statues in Trafalgar Square

George IV was the Prince Regent before he became king. Regent Street is named after him. His statue shows him riding bareback.

Statue of George IV

The statue of Charles I on horseback looks down Whitehall. Charles I was the only English king to have been executed.

Statue of Charles I

Shopping

Shopping in London can be a very varied experience. These are just a few of the famous places you can visit.

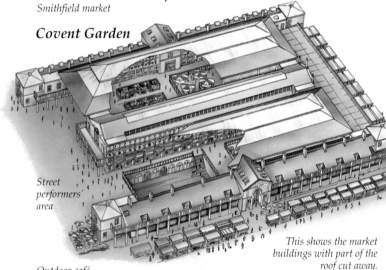

Bobbing hat

Billingsgate and Smithfield markets

Billingsgate and Smithfield markets are two of the oldest traditional wholesale markets in London.

Smithfield market

Smithfield market sells meat and Billingsgate sells fish. They both start very early, at 5am.

Some of the market porters at Billingsgate market wear flat, hard hats called bobbing hats to carry boxes.

Covent Garden

Street performers' area

This shows the market buildings with part of the roof cut away.

Outdoor café in the Piazza

Covent Garden is one of London's most famous shopping areas. It started as a convent garden where monks sold the vegetables they didn't need. Now it has restaurants, market stalls and boutiques.

Oxford Street

Oxford Street is seen as the main shopping street in London. Most major stores have branches there. Around Christmas time, the whole area is packed with people, and has spectacular street decorations.

Christmas decorations

Hamleys

Hamleys on Regent Street is the world's largest toy store. It has six floors packed with thousands of different toys, and you can see working mechanical toys around the store.

Hamleys toy store

Harrods

Harrods in Knightsbridge is probably the most famous store in London, and it is the largest department store in Europe. It has over 300 departments, including its well-known food halls which sell a huge variety of food.

Harrods

Special events

Whatever time of year you visit London, there are special events to watch or take part in. Many are based on old traditions.

Notting Hill Carnival

This Caribbean-style carnival takes place in August around the Portobello Road area of Notting Hill. It is very lively with lots of decorated floats, dancing and reggae groups.

Pearly Harvest Festival

In September, the Pearly families (see page 30) hold a Harvest Festival in St. Martin-in-the-Fields church. You can see them outside in their costumes after the service.

Sporting events

One of the world's most famous tennis tournaments is held in Wimbledon at the end of June.

A ladies' singles match at Wimbledon

Wimbledon is famous for strawberries and cream and its special atmosphere as well as the tennis.

The Oxford and Cambridge boat race

Oxford and Cambridge Universities have a traditional boat race each Easter on the Thames. The Cambridge boat has light blue oars and Oxford has dark blue ones.

Trooping the Colour

Trooping the Colour

This ceremony celebrates the Queen's official birthday each June. She attends a procession on Horse Guards' Parade where different military regiments parade their regimental flags. These flags are known as "colours".

The Lord Mayor's Show

The City area of London has its own Lord Mayor. A new one is elected each year and is sworn in during the Lord Mayor's Show, which happens each November. The new Mayor travels to the ceremony in a magnificent red and gold coach.

The Lord Mayor's procession

Christmas and New Year

Each year Norway sends Britain a Christmas tree in thanks for wartime help. It stands in Trafalgar Square and the lights are turned on by the Ambassador of Norway.

On New Year's Eve thousands of people gather in Trafalgar Square to greet the New Year.

The Chinese community celebrates New Year in January or February. There is a procession through Chinatown, Soho, led by a figure of a dancing lion who is supposed to frighten away evil spirits.

Famous people

Every city has its heroes and heroines and also its villains. London is no exception. These are just some of the people who have been important in London's history.

The Globe Theatre

William Shakespeare

Shakespeare spent much of his life in London. His plays were performed at the Globe Theatre on the South Bank, which has recently been rebuilt.

Children celebrating on November 5

Guy Fawkes

At midnight on November 4, 1605, Guy Fawkes was found in the Houses of Parliament. He was about to set light to barrels of gunpowder. He was executed, and his capture is still celebrated on November 5 each year.

Samuel Pepys

Samuel Pepys lived in London in the seventeenth century. His diaries tell us a lot about London at that time. They include accounts of the Plague and the Great Fire of London (see page 7).

Londoner quiz

During your visit, see if you can find answers to these questions:

Where is there a bust of Karl Marx?

Why did Emmeline Pankhurst chain herself to the railings of 10 Downing Street?

What are the Kray Twins famous for?

What did William Hogarth do for a living?

The answers are on page 32.

22

Florence Nightingale

Florence Nightingale is best known for her work as a nurse among soldiers in the Crimean War. However, she also made improvements to the way that London hospitals were run, and set up two training schools for nurses.

A statue of Florence Nightingale in Waterloo Place, Pall Mall

Charles Dickens

Charles Dickens is one of London's most famous writers. He wrote about the hard lives that many people led in Victorian times.

Sir Robert Peel

Sir Robert Peel was a nineteenth century Prime Minister. He founded the London Police Force. Policemen were sometimes called "bobbies" or "peelers" after him.

A nineteenth century policeman or "peeler"

Sir Winston Churchill

Churchill is probably the most famous Prime Minister of Britain this century. He led the country during the Second World War and became well-known for his encouraging speeches. There is a statue of him at Westminster, looking over toward the Houses of Parliament.

Sir Winston Churchill

Mysteries and tragedies

London's long, varied history has many tales of intrigue and horror attached to it. The Tower of London probably has the most, but there are plenty of others from all over the city.

The Princes in the Tower

In 1483 the young King Edward V and his even younger brother the Duke of York were imprisoned in the Bloody Tower by their uncle Richard, who then became Richard III. After a while they disappeared. Nobody knows for sure what happened to them, but the bones of two boys were found in the Tower in the 1600s. Most people think that Richard had them murdered.

People claimed to see the boys' ghosts before their bones were found.

Anne Boleyn

One of the most tragic executions at the Tower of London was that of Anne Boleyn, Henry VIII's second wife. When she did not give birth to a baby boy, he accused her of being unfaithful and had her beheaded. Unlike other prisoners at the Tower, she was executed with a sword.

Anne Boleyn

Lady Jane Grey

Lady Jane Grey was another tragic victim on Tower Green. She was beheaded in 1554, when she had been queen for just nine days. She was only sixteen when she died.

The horrific tools of the executioner at the Tower of London

The ghost at Hampton Court

Catherine Howard, Henry VIII's fifth wife, is said to haunt the part of Hampton Court now known as the Haunted Gallery. When she had been condemned to death, she tried to reach Henry to beg for mercy while he was at Mass. She pounded on the chapel door but she was not allowed in.

The guards dragged Catherine Howard away from the chapel door screaming.

Cleopatra's Needle

This Egyptian monument on Victoria Embankment is 3,500 years old. It had a terrible journey to London in the 1870s in which six sailors died. Some people claim that a mysterious figure occasionally comes out of the shadows nearby and jumps into the river, but nobody ever hears a splash.

Jack the Ripper

Jack the Ripper was a murderer who terrorized London in 1888. All six victims were women who were gruesomely murdered in the Spitalfields area. He was never caught, and his identity is still a mystery.

The Theatre Royal, Drury Lane

It is said that a lucky ghost haunts the Theatre Royal, appearing only during successful productions. In Victorian times, a skeleton was found in a bricked-up room with a dagger between its ribs. This might explain why the ghost appears, but not why it is lucky.

Stories and songs

These are stories and songs that have become almost legendary in the history of London.

Dick Whittington

The story goes that Dick Whittington was a poor boy who walked to London to find his fortune. He got a job as a cook's boy, and bought a cat. However, the cook treated him badly, so he left his cat and set out for home. As he reached the edge of London the Bow bells rang, "Turn again Dick Whittington, thrice Lord Mayor of London". So he turned back. Meanwhile, his cat had boarded a ship and killed a plague of rats in a distant country, so an emperor bought it. This made Dick wealthy, and he became Lord Mayor of London three times.

Dick Whittington and his cat

Oliver Twist

Of all Charles Dickens's stories set in London, Oliver Twist is the best-known. It tells the tale of a young boy in Victorian times who has to beg and steal for a living until someone kind takes care of him. Like many of Dickens's stories, it showed what life was really like for the poor in London and eventually led to changes being made to help them.

Sherlock Holmes

Sherlock Holmes was a fictional Victorian detective created by Sir Arthur Conan Doyle. In the stories, he lived at 221B Baker Street and solved many crimes in the city's underworld. He was helped by his assistant, Dr. Watson.

"Oranges and lemons"

This is a famous old song about churches in the City of London.

St. Clement Danes

Oranges and lemons,
Say the bells of St. Clement's.
You owe me five farthings,
Say the bells of St. Martin's.
When will you pay me?
Say the bells of Old Bailey.
When I grow rich,
Say the bells of Shoreditch.
When will that be?
Say the bells of Stepney.
I do not know,
Says the great bell of Bow.

St. Mary-le-Bow

"Pussy cat, pussy cat, where have you been?"

This old nursery rhyme is said to be about Queen Elizabeth I.

Pussy cat, pussy cat, where have you been?
I've been to London to see the Queen.
Pussy cat, pussy cat, what did you there?
I frightened a little mouse under her chair.

Queen Elizabeth I

"London Bridge is falling down"

There are many ideas about the story behind this song. One possibility is that it was based on a poem written after a battle between Anglo-Saxons and Danish Vikings in 1014, in which London Bridge was pulled down.

London Bridge is falling down,
Falling down, falling down,
London Bridge is falling down,
My fair lady!

Things to do

There are lots of different things that you can pack into even a short visit to London.

Boat trips on the Thames

Tower Bridge

A riverboat approaching Tower Bridge

You can go on sightseeing trips along the River Thames from Westminster, Charing Cross and Tower Piers. Some trips go east toward the Tower Bridge, Greenwich and the Thames Barrier. Others go west to Richmond and Hampton Court.

Exploring Greenwich

The line between the world's eastern and western hemispheres runs through Greenwich, at the Old Royal Observatory. Greenwich Mean Time is worked out from this line, and all the different times around the world are based on this.

Standing on the line at the Old Royal Observatory

You can explore the Cutty Sark, which is a "clipper" in dry dock at Greenwich. It was launched in 1869. Clippers were the fastest ships in the nineteenth century. The Cutty Sark was used to carry tea from China to England.

28

Walks and bus trips

You can go on guided walks around parts of the city. Many have special themes.

Open-top sightseeing bus

Some guides are trained by the London Tourist Board. They are called Blue Badge Guides.

To get a good view of London, you can take a sightseeing bus which goes on an interesting route around the city.

Activities in parks

Rowing on the Serpentine in Hyde Park

In Hyde Park, you can hire rowing boats on the Serpentine at some times of year. People also go riding along Rotten Row. This name comes from *Route du Roi*, which is French for King's Road.

Regent's Canal runs through Regent's Park. You can take narrowboat trips along it between Camden Lock and Little Venice.

Indian elephants at London Zoo

Narrowboats on Regent's Canal

You can visit London Zoo in Regent's Park, which keeps over 12,000 animals from all over the world. Some of them are very rare.

Entertainment

There are always plenty of shows and concerts to choose from. You can find out what's on by buying the magazine *Time Out*, available from newsagents.

A play being performed in Regent's Park

Living in London

London is very cosmopolitan, which means that people from many different cultures live there. This makes it difficult to describe what life is like for everyone in the city, but there are some things which are fairly typical.

Chinatown in Soho is an example of London's mix of different cultures.

Where people live

Many people who work in London live in the suburbs, others even farther out of London.

A typical street in a London suburb

Some people live in unusual places such as houseboats on the Thames.

People living in more central areas often live in flats or apartments. Many of the tall houses built in the eighteenth century have now been turned into flats.

Pearly families

A Pearly King and Queen

Pearly families were originally the leaders of Victorian costermongers, or street traders. Being a Pearly is an inherited position, so Pearly families still exist. The head of each family is a "King" or "Queen". On special occasions they wear costumes covered in pearl buttons, which is how they got their name.

Cockney rhyming slang

A Cockney is a true Londoner – traditionally someone born within the sound of the bells of St. Mary-le-Bow (the Bow bells) in the City (see page 4). Cockney rhyming slang developed in Victorian times. It works by replacing words with other rhyming words.

Mince pies = eyes
Dicky Dirt = shirt
Tit for tat = hat
Plates of meat = feet
Whistle and flute = suit
North and south = mouth
Loaf of bread = head
Hampstead Heath = teeth

People to look out for

Newspaper vendors sell evening newspapers from little booths, often near Tube stations.

London policemen often wear tall helmets, developed from the top hats they used to wear.

Couriers deliver urgent packages around the city on bicycles or motorcycles.

Chelsea Pensioners are old soldiers who wear a scarlet uniform with a black hat.

Modern street traders still sell fruit and vegetables from barrows on the street.

City workers wear suits. The men used to wear bowler hats, but this is rare now.

The bright lights of Piccadilly Circus have come to represent life in London at night. Londoners as well as tourists gather in the West End to find entertainment.

Index

Answers to the quiz on page 22: 1) Highgate Cemetery 2) To protest against women not being allowed to vote, early in the 20th century 3) The Kray Twins were notorious criminals in the East End 4) Hogarth was a famous painter in the 18th century.

Additional illustrations: Guy Smith, Peter Dennis, Gerald Wood, Peter Bull, Martin Newton and Elaine Lee

This book is based on material previously published in The Usborne Book of London, The Usborne Book of Kings & Queens, The Usborne Book of Britain, Essential British History, The Cats Sticker Book and The Usborne Guide to the Supernatural World.

First published in 1996 by Usborne Publishing Ltd, 83-85 Saffron Hill, London EC1N 8RT, England. Copyright © Usborne Publishing Ltd 1978, 1979, 1980, 1985, 1987, 1990, 1991, 1992, 1993, 1994, 1995, 1996.